This Book Belongs To:

_____

Date & Grade:

_____

CELEBRATING 5 YEARS OF HOG MOLLIES BOOKS!

The past five years, The 2nd & 7 Foundation has visited hundreds of schools while highlighting some valuable lessons in our books. Sharing our stories each week with so many children has been a fun way to help us reach our goal of Tackling Illiteracy. We hope you enjoy these books as much as we have enjoyed seeing the smiling faces in each classroom we visit.

Since this is the 5th year anniversary for The Hog Mollies series of books, we would like to recognize all those responsible for helping The 2nd & 7 Foundation grow:

- The Hog Mollies Writing Crew (Amy Hoying, Leah Miller & Jason Tharp)
- The Ohio State University Department of Athletics
- Participating Elementary School Teachers & Principals
- Current and Former OSU Student-Athlete Readers
- High School Student-Athlete Readers
- FUNdamental Football Camp Participants & Volunteers
- 8-Ball Shootout Participants & Volunteers
- Friends of The 2nd & 7 Foundation
- Interns from The Ohio State University
- Our Major Sponsors (White Castle, KeyBank, Roosters & Giant Eagle)
- Countless Individual Donors

Thank you again for sharing our passion for literacy.
We can't wait for the next five Hog Mollies adventures!

Luke Fickell   Ryan Miller   Mike Vrabel

Cover and Interior Illustrations © 2012 Jason Tharp
The Hog Mollies & The Camp Carmen Campfire. Copyright © 2012 by The 2nd and 7 Foundation

ISBN 978-0-4652-0590-2
ISBN 978-0-4652-0604-6

Production Date: 05/09/14
Batch numbers: 430590-02
Printed by: Walsworth, Marceline, MO; United States of America

10 9 8 7 6 5 4 3 2   16 15 14

SECONDANDSEVEN
FOUNDATION

WHAT WE DO

WHO WE ARE

The mission of The 2nd & 7 Foundation is to promote literacy by providing free books and positive role models for kids in need.

OUR PROGRAM
The purpose of The 2nd & 7 Foundation is to promote children's literacy in central Ohio and across the country. We have created the "Tackle Illiteracy" program to reach out to the children in our community to reinforce the importance of reading. Each week during the school year, we travel with varsity student-athletes from The Ohio State University to central Ohio elementary schools to read to the entire 2nd grade class. After we discuss the message in the book and the importance of reading, we give each student a book to take home. Across the country, we ship our books, for free, to schools and programs that need the most support.

The 2nd & 7 Foundation is an organization located in Columbus, Ohio, developed around the idea of giving back to the community. Three former Ohio State University student-athletes who played football for the Buckeyes - Luke Fickell, Mike Vrabel, and Ryan Miller - were inspired to start a foundation after being involved in various community service activities while at OSU. Their passion for helping those less fortunate paved the way for the creation of The 2nd & 7 Foundation. The former Buckeyes knew that they could make a difference by helping kids see the importance of reading in order to have a successful future.

Mike Vrabel

Ryan Miller

OUR GOAL
We have made it our goal to donate a minimum of 10,000 new books to children each year. Our program now touches every 2nd grade student in Columbus City Schools thanks to the generosity of the community and our sponsors.

Luke Fickell

The Hog Mollies

and the
Camp Carmen
Campfire

Written by: The 2nd & 7 Foundation
Illustrated by: Jason Tharp

SECONDANDSEVEN
FOUNDATION

Kendall Hunt
publishing company
4050 Westmark Drive • P O Box 1840 • Dubuque IA 52004-1840

It was an early summer morning when Duke woke up to the CLICKETY-CLANK of Uncle Archie's old pickup truck.

Duke's stomach turned. Although he was excited to spend the week outdoors with his friends, he couldn't stop thinking about his last camping trip.

As he threw his gear into the truck, Duke saw that his best friends Sprout, Harley, and Hoppy were loaded up and ready to go. "Alright Hog Mollies, I hope you've all been practicing your camping skills," Uncle Archie said.

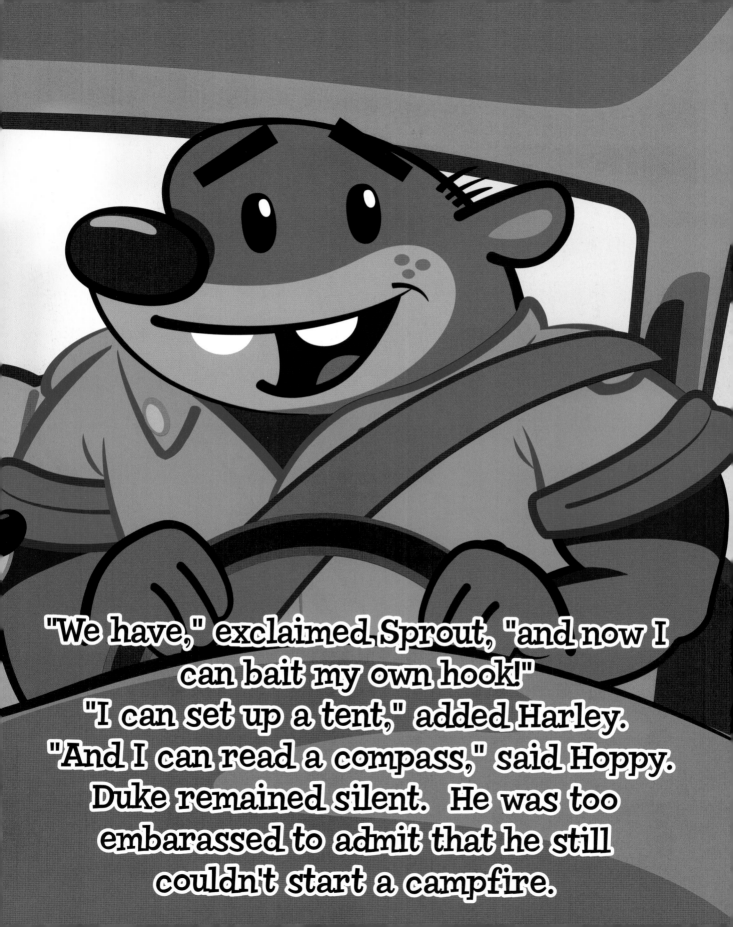

"We have," exclaimed Sprout, "and now I can bait my own hook!"
"I can set up a tent," added Harley.
"And I can read a compass," said Hoppy.
Duke remained silent. He was too embarassed to admit that he still couldn't start a campfire.

Upon arrival at Camp Carmen, Uncle Archie assigned each Hog Mollie a task.

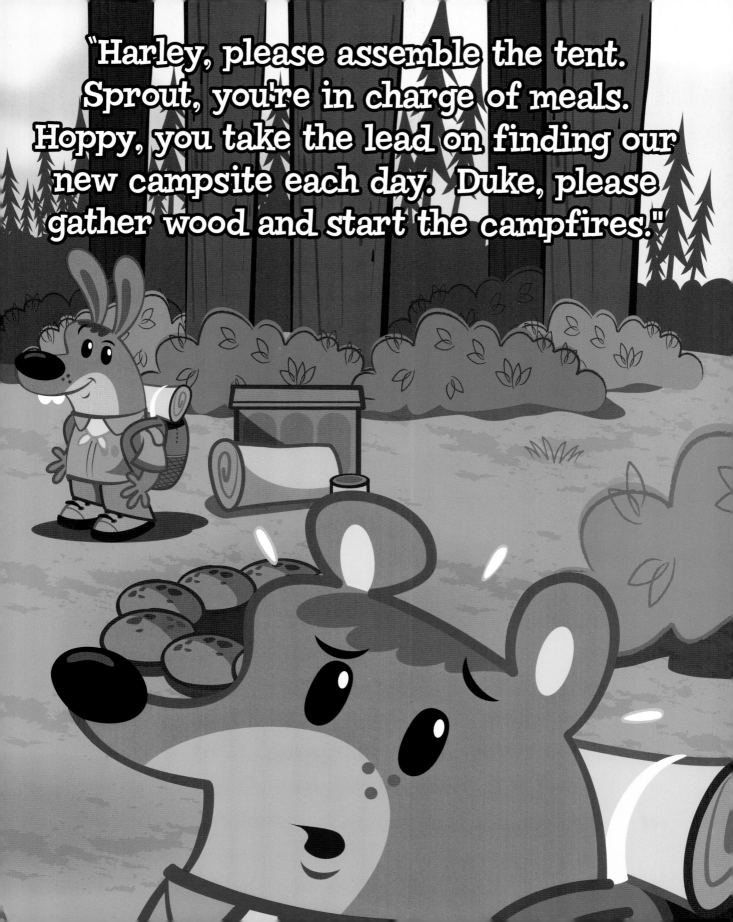

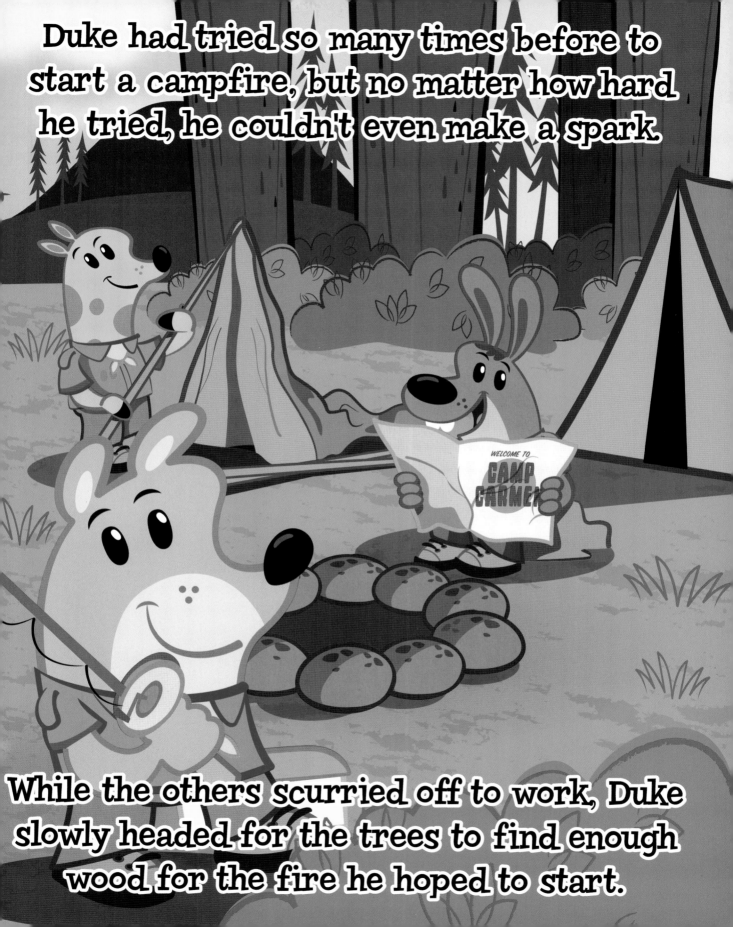

Duke had tried so many times before to start a campfire, but no matter how hard he tried, he couldn't even make a spark.

While the others scurried off to work, Duke slowly headed for the trees to find enough wood for the fire he hoped to start.

Down at the river, Sprout was having trouble getting even a nibble on his line. Instead of getting frustrated, he thought of Uncle Archie's wise words and recast his line a bit further downstream.

Wow! Uncle Archie was right, he thought. *We'll have a fish feast tonight!*

Back at the campsite, Duke was getting upset. He had been rubbing two sticks together for what seemed like hours, and was starting to lose his patience.

Hoppy noticed Duke's frustration and offered to help. Within a few minutes, he had a roaring fire. "How did you do that, Hoppy? I'll never be able to start one on my own," Duke lamented.

"It takes PATIENCE, PRACTICE & PERSISTENCE, just like Uncle Archie always says," Hoppy replied. "Don't give up. I know you can do it!"

For the next few days, the Hog Mollies enjoyed fishing, hiking and exchanging stories around the campfire.

Everything seemed perfect, but Duke was not happy. Each night, he needed help to start the fire.

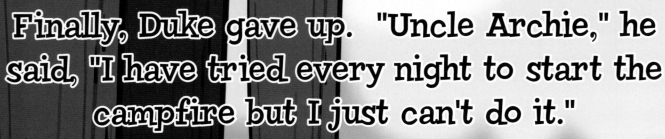

Finally, Duke gave up. "Uncle Archie," he said, "I have tried every night to start the campfire but I just can't do it."

"Duke, when I was a young camper I got lost all the time," Uncle Archie told him. "My grandfather gave me a compass and told me to use PATIENCE, PRACTICE & PERSISTENCE when trying to find my way."

"Unfortunately, I didn't always listen to him. One day when I was lost and frustrated I threw my compass into the trees near the river and never saw it again. Now I understand what he was trying to teach me, and I wish I had that compass as a reminder."

That night, Duke told his friends the story of Uncle Archie's compass. "Wouldn't it be great if we could find his compass to thank him for taking us camping?" Duke asked.

The Hog Mollies agreed and decided to set out on a search for it the next day.

After hours of searching and climbing and digging and exploring, the Hog Mollies found Uncle Archie's compass. "Look," said Duke, "it says something on the back!"

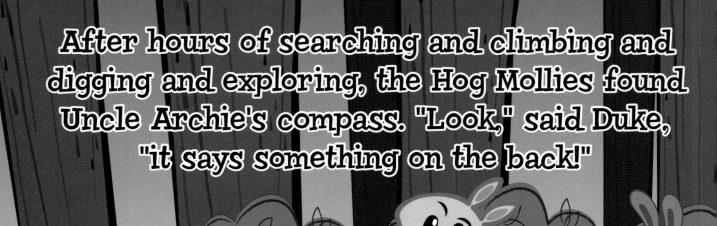

The Hog Mollies couldn't wait to show Uncle Archie what they found, but the sun was setting and they began hearing unfamiliar noises. "Guys, I'm getting scared," said Hoppy. "I think we're lost and there's no way I can get us back in the dark" "What should we do?" asked Sprout. "And where's Duke?"

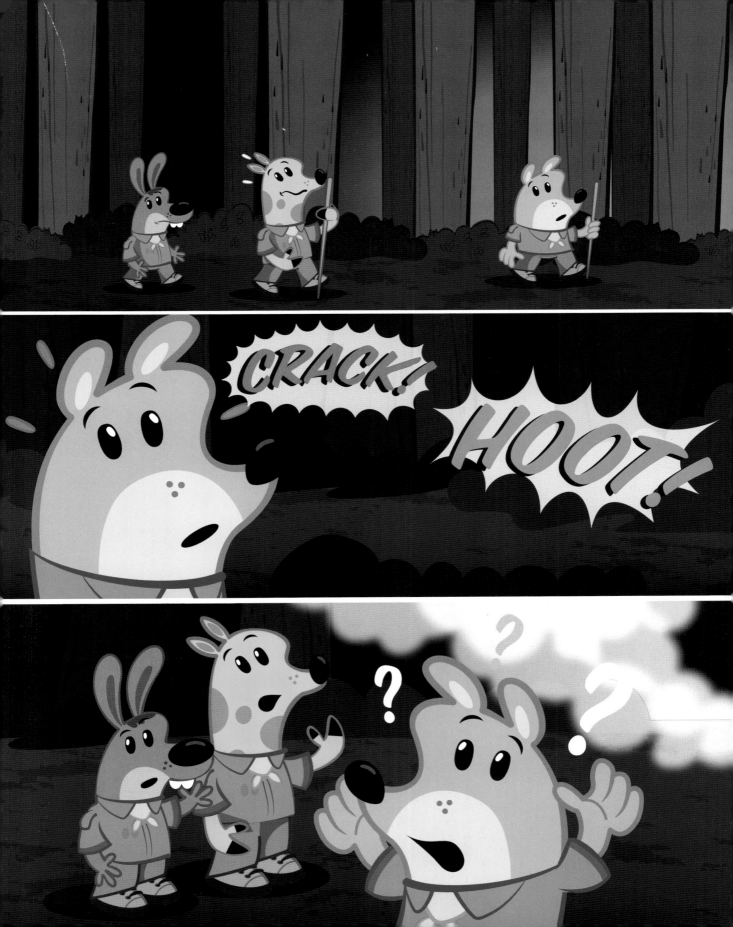

There he is!

Duke, you started a campfire!

Way to go!

"I thought about what Uncle Archie said and I didn't want to give up. Let's just stay close to the fire for the night and we can find him in the morning," Duke said.

"Not if I find you first!" exclaimed Uncle Archie. "I saw the smoke from the fire. It looks like Duke's

PATIENCE, PRACTICE & PERSISTENCE

has paid off."

"And look what we found, Uncle Archie!"
Duke exclaimed

PATIENCE
PRACTICE
PERSISTENCE

"Thank you for helping us find our way."

How to Make Buckeye S'mores

Ingredients:

- Graham Crackers
- Marshmallows
- Peanut Butter
- Chocolate Bars

**With help from a grown-up,
roast marshmallows over a fire.**

Take one large graham cracker and break it in half (one for top cracker and one for bottom cracker). Spread peanut butter on top of one graham cracker half and top with a square of chocolate. Place your roasted marshmallow on top of the peanut butter and chocolate and press down with the remaining half of the graham cracker.

Enjoy with a story around the campfire!

I used patience, practice and persistence when . . .

_____

_____

_____

_____

_____

_____

_____

_____